## Dedication

For my ancestors: I thank you for surviving when so many did not. You make me proud of who I am because of who you were.

George Littlechild

George Littlechild

(1991)

Rachel Littlechild
my mother
(1940s)

Edward Littlechild
my grandfather
(1915)

Bella Bull
my grandmother
(1916)

Alexander Littlechild
my great-grandfather
(1920s)

Jenny Cardinal
my great-grandmother
(1910)

Chief Francis Bull
my great-grandfather
(1930s)

Peggy Louis Natuasis
my great-grandmother
(1890s)

Chief Louis Bull
my great-great-
grandfather (1920s)

Mariann Sikak
my great-great-
grandmother (1905)

Louis Natuasis
my great-great-
grandfather (1898)

Betsy Samson
my great-great-
grandmother (1940s)

*(Dates indicate when photographs were taken.)*

# This Land Is My Land

# George Littlechild

**Children's Book Press** ⟳ *an imprint of* **Lee & Low Books Inc.**
**New York**

# I LOVE THE MOON, THE STARS, AND THE ANCESTORS

 I paint at night. I'm inspired to paint at night. I stand outside staring at the night sky and I begin to dream. The sky is like a doorway into the other world, the Spirit World.

I am inspired by the ancestors. When I look back on our history and see all the difficulties our ancestors had to face, I can only honor them. Through the wisdom of our Elders and the courage of all our people we have survived the past 500 years. I thank the Creator for *Wahkomkanak*, our ancestors.

In the center of this picture is Chief Joseph Samson. He wears an eagle headdress, the highest symbol in our culture. On the top and the sides of the picture are images of my great-great-grandfather, Louis Natuasis, who lived from 1858 to 1926. He was a headman to Chief Joseph Samson. He was born when my people were still free, when the buffalo still roamed.

In those days our Nation, the Plains Cree people, followed the buffalo in the spring and summer. In the winter we made camp by the rivers, which were the ancient roadways. The trees protected us from the snows and the winds. We hid in the valleys from our traditional enemies, the Blackfoot people.

# COLUMBUS FIRST SAW

When Columbus came to the Americas 500 years ago, he looked at the people he saw and called us "Indians" because he was on the way to India. The man in my painting is looking at Columbus and he is totally surprised. I, too, would have been surprised if I had been there. "Who are these men whose skin is so pale? Have they come from the Spirit World to guide us? What do they want, these men who are not like us?"

I remember hearing about Columbus at school when I was a boy. The teacher said he was a great man because he had discovered America. Even then I wondered how Columbus could have discovered America when my people were already here.

Since Columbus came to the Americas, my people have lost most of our land and we have suffered much. Knowing what I do now about our history, I would have offered Columbus a meal and a place to stay and treated him as a guest, but I would not have allowed him to take away our land.

## DOT THE "I" IN NORTH AMERICAN INDIAN

When I was a boy the teacher always made us dot the "i." She would smack the chalk against the board and a cloud of chalk dust would fly up. From that time on I knew you had to have respect for the letter "i." The word "Indian" has two "i"s. At the bottom of the painting, there are *lots* of "i"s.

The arrow in the night sky points to the railroad that brought the white people westward. The white men wanted to own the land they lived on, which meant that we could not share it. Indians never owned the land. Nothing belonged to us. Everything we had, we shared. So when the white men came we found their ways very unusual.

## MOUNTIE AND INDIAN CHIEF

This picture brings you face to face with two different cultures. The Mountie is a Royal Canadian Mounted Policeman sent by the Queen of England and the Government of Canada to enforce the law of the Europeans. The Chief is a leader of the Plains Cree. He is protecting our people and our way of life.

But our way of life was being destroyed. The white men were taking more and more of our land. They put us onto reserves, which were just little pieces of the territory we used to have; and we couldn't come or go without their permission. My ancestors must have cried much as they became prisoners on their own land.

## FOUR BUFFALO SPIRITS

The mighty buffalo fed and clothed my ancestors. Millions of these magnificent animals once roamed the plains. By the end of the 1800s they were almost extinct — killed for money by the white men. This extermination was devastating to my ancestors who depended upon the buffalo for their very survival.

I painted four buffalo because four is a sacred number. These four represent the millions who have died. Four is also a healing number. It appears in all my work. There are four directions, four seasons, four elements, and four kinds of animals (those who walk, those who fly, those who swim, and those who crawl.)

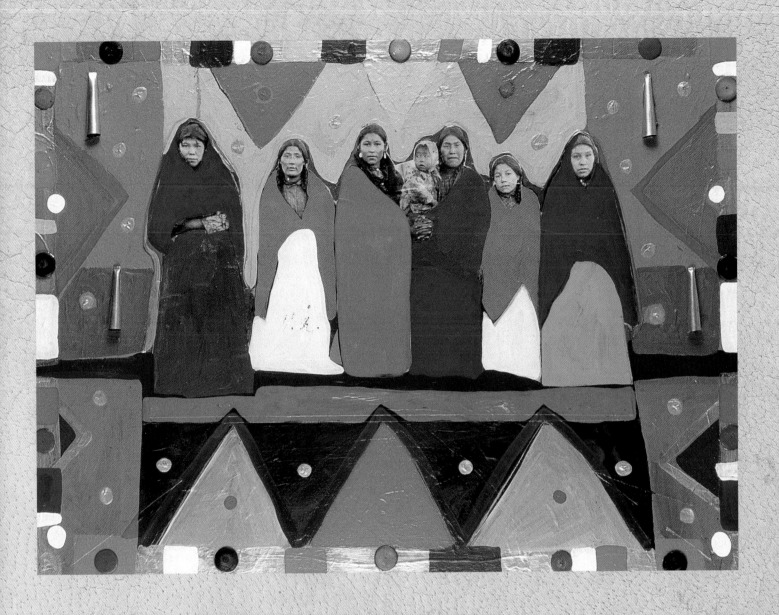

## GIVE THANKS TO THE GRANDMOTHERS

I have a fear of mountains. I'm scared of closed-in spaces like those spaces in between the mountains, because I grew up on the plains where it's flat.

When I first came to Vancouver, I had to drive through the mountains for 12 hours. My understanding cousin accompanied me on the trip. After we made it to our destination, my cousin said, "Give thanks to the Grandmothers for our safe passage." I have learned about respecting the Grandmothers and Grand-fathers, the ancestors who have gone on to the Spirit World. I have learned that I can pray to them and that they will help guide me, just as the Creator does. My Great-Grandmother, Peggy Louis Natuasis, stands third from the left.

# URBAN INDIAN PAIN DANCE

 My brother Raymond has magical eyes. They're like husky dogs' eyes. There is no other green like this. They are not like Caucasian eyes or Indian eyes. My brother is a mixed blood, and so am I. Our mother, Rachel Littlechild was Plains Cree. Our father, James E. Price, was Scottish, French, English, Micmac Indian, Welsh, and Dutch. We come from the spirit of two peoples.

Urban Indian Pain Dance is about the pain of our history. After the Second World War, many of us left the reserves and tried to find jobs in the cities. But there were no jobs, and so some of us got caught up in drugs, alcohol, and prostitution. My brothers and sisters and I were raised by the welfare because both our parents died violent deaths on skid row. Living in the cities was like being in prison because we had lost control of our lives. That's why I put bars in the background of this picture.

My brother Raymond overcame all the hardships. He succeeded against tremendous odds. He stayed in school. He went on to the University and earned a degree. Now he works in business management and is greatly respected. He is proud of being an Indian and he is helping to give the next generation the opportunities that he never had. For me, working as an artist is my way of healing the pain of the past and helping the next generation of Indian people.

# IN MEMORY OF THE SIOUX WARRIORS

 This painting of a horse spirit honors the Sioux warriors who died at the Battle of Little Big Horn. It is a memorial piece to Indigenous people who fought and died for their land.

Like the Sioux, my ancestors were Plains Indians. We hunted the buffalo. We rode horses. The horse is a sacred animal for us. In this picture, Horse's clothing moves as if he wants to dance. Bright happy colors of the rainbow adorn him. The star emblem in the middle of his chest represents the morning star. This star slowly fades away at the break of dawn, welcoming the beginning of a new day.

The little pink and purple horses in the background come from the toy store. Do you know those bags of plastic cowboys and Indians on horses you can buy? These are those same horses.

# THIS LAND IS MY LAND

 When I was a boy I was taught the song "This land is your land, this land is my land." When I got older I thought it was very strange to be singing about the ownership of the land. Whose land was this? Did it belong to anyone? The first people in this land were the Indians. We prefer to be called First Nations or First Peoples, because this was our homeland first.

North America is a very large continent. Add Central America and South America and together they make up the whole Western Hemisphere. This painting reminds us that all this land was once Indian land.

# RED HORSE BOARDING SCHOOL

 For many years, up through the 1960s, the government took Indian children away from their families and forced us to live in boarding schools. If our parents hid us or refused to let the Indian agent take us away, they were jailed.

In these places we "Red Indians" as we were called were educated in the white man's way. The teachers forced us to learn English and become Christians. They cut off our braided hair, they beat us if we spoke our Indian languages. We suffered much cruelty and abuse. They even numbered us—can you imagine being called "Number 29" instead of your name?

In my picture the red horse is torn in half because Indian children coming to the school were torn away from their culture, their language, their traditional ways, and their families. My mother and all her brothers and sisters went to these boarding schools, and so did my grandparents. They grew up without their families and never learned how to raise children of their own. Many boarding school survivors died on skid row of alcoholism, including my mother.

I used gold stars in the sky and on the roof because they remind me of my school experience. My teachers would grade us by using stars. The gold stars were for the best students. The lowest stars were red, which meant failure. Those are the stars I remember getting most.

# RED HORSE IN A SEA OF WHITE HORSES

After my parents died, I was taken in by a white family, and I went to an all–white school. It wasn't easy. The white students used to call me a "fat, ugly, stupid Indian." I didn't even know what an Indian was. I heard this every day and when I didn't hear it I imagined it. Eventually I believed I was all those things they said about me. Now that I've grown up, I know that those people were wrong.

In this picture, an Indian warrior sits atop a red horse. Not at home in his own territory, this red horse lives among the white horses who find him different and don't understand him. The red horse is taught that he is always wrong and whites are always right. That is why the check marks appear on the white horses.

The red horse represents me.

**HORSE DANCE**

My great-grandfather, Chief Francis Bull, had a great love and respect for horses, and these animals also loved and respected him.

## A DANCING BIRD SEEKS FREEDOM

    I once lived in a house where there were birds in a cage.
I used to listen to them sing and watch them fly about in their
tiny home. Then one day one of the birds ended up in one of
my paintings. She wanted freedom.

## WINNER OF THE MISS HOBBEMA INDIAN PRINCESS PAGEANT

This picture is about a celebration for a young woman presenting herself to the community. Her outfit has been made by the Grandmothers, who love her very much. It represents the four elements: earth, air, water, and fire. The dress is made from animal hide, which represents Mother Earth. The feathers are from the air. The shells are from the water. The fire is her spirit. During the pageant she will thank everyone in the community, especially the grandmothers, for all that they have given her.

My intention in this painting is to break down stereotypes and help restore a sense of dignity, pride, and elegance to the women of the Plains Cree.

# INDIAN ARTIST VISITS NEW YORK, NEW YORK

This painting is about my first visit to New York City. What a great time I had! I loved the tall buildings, the crowds of people, the huge stores, the fancy restaurants. And the art! It was amazing. There were paintings that had photographs in them. Others had fabric and buttons. There were paintings on canvas with wood and straw.

When I returned home I began to experiment with mixed media. My paintings became multi–layered, with beads, feathers, and photographs. In ten days my world had changed.

Yes, that is a photograph of me, standing ever so small beside the large towers.

## DANCING BUFFALO

Can you imagine a buffalo dancing?  Better yet, can you imagine millions of buffalo dancing?

Are buffalo fuschia-pink and gold?  Of course not, but sometimes it's good not to be so serious.  It's good medicine to laugh.

 This young traditional warrior is on his way to a pow wow.  He holds his head up proudly.  He's off to go dancing.  To dance is to celebrate life.  With each beat of the drum we celebrate the heartbeat of Mother Earth.

My people dance at pow wows.  We have jingle-dress dancers, who are girls and women.  We have fancy dancers, who can be men, women, or children.  Boys and men are grass dancers and chicken dancers and do the sneak-up dance.  The Elders and the traditionalists dance traditional dances, all together in a large circle.

The circle is a very important symbol to all Indians because the circle represents strength and unity.  When we say the circle has been broken, we mean that our culture has been tampered with.  In Indian Country we are closing the circle by healing ourselves.  We are reviving our culture and traditions.  We are very hopeful and the future looks promising.

**George Littlechild** is an artist of international renown. He is a member of the Plains Cree Nation, which is part of the Cree Nation, the largest Indian nation in Canada. His work is celebrated for its exciting use of color, its themes from his Plains Cree background, and its spirit of playfulness. His paintings have been shown in galleries across Canada, in the United States, and in Europe and Japan. They can be found in many public and private collections.

Littlechild was born in Edmonton, Alberta in 1958, and spent his first four years living on and off the reserve at Hobbema, Alberta. He grew up in Edmonton and received his Bachelor of Fine Arts degree from the Nova Scotia College of Arts and Design in Halifax, Nova Scotia. He currently lives in Vancouver, British Columbia.

Children's Book Press is grateful to the Pacific Telesis Foundation and the BankAmerica Foundation whose generous donations supported the publication of *This Land Is My Land*.

Photograph in painting on page 21 by Edward Curtis, courtesy of the Glen Bow Museum, Calgary, Alberta.

Book design: Mira Reisberg
Book production: The Kids at Our House
Book editors: Harriet Rohmer, David Schecter
Cover lettering: Lily Lee
Thanks to Larry Garfinkle for his cooperation. Thanks to Maryanne Palmer for her help.

Library of Congress Cataloging-in-Publication Data
Littlechild, George.
This land is my land / George Littlechild.   p.   cm.
Summary: Using text and his own paintings, the author describes the experiences of Indians of North America in general as well as his experiences growing up as a Plains Cree Indian in Canada.
ISBN 978-0-89239-184-4 (paperback)
1. Littlechild, George—Juvenile literature. 2. Cree Indians—Biography—Juvenile literature. [1. Littlechild, George.
2. Cree Indians—Biography. 3. Indians of North America.] I. Title.
E99.C88L575   1993   971'.004973'0092—dc20  [6]        93-12932  CIP AC

FSC
www.fsc.org
MIX
Paper from responsible sources
FSC® C020691

Manufactured in China by Jade Productions, June 2016
10  9  8  7  6  5
First Edition